A Note to Parents

DK READERS is a compelling program for beginning readers, designed in conjunction with leading literacy experts, including Dr. Linda Gambrell, Distinguished Professor of Education at Clemson University. Dr. Gambrell has served as President of the National Reading Conference, the College Reading Association, and the International Reading Association.

Beautiful illustrations and superb full-color photographs combine with engaging, easy-to-read stories to offer a fresh approach to each subject in the series. Each DK READER is guaranteed to capture a child's interest while developing his or her reading skills, general knowledge, and love of reading.

The five levels of DK READERS are aimed at different reading abilities, enabling you to choose the books that are exactly right for your child:

Pre-level 1: Learning to read
Level 1: Beginning to read
Level 2: Beginning to read alone
Level 3: Reading alone
Level 4: Proficient readers

D1111847

The "normal" age at which a child begins to read can be anywhere from three to eight years old. Adult participation through the lower levels is very helpful for providing encouragement, discussing storylines, and sounding out unfamiliar words.

No matter which level you select, you can be sure that you are helping your child learn to read, then read to learn!

DK | Penguin Random House

Project Editor Lara Tankel Holtz
Art Editor Susan Calver
Senior Editor Linda Esposito
Publishing Manager Bridget Giles
US Editor Regina Kahney
Production Editor Marc Staples
Picture Research Jo Carlill
Photographer Lynton Gardiner
Jacket Designer Mary Sandberg

Reading Consultant
Linda B. Gambrell, Ph.D.

First American Edition, 1998
This edition, 2011
Published in the United States by DK Publishing
345 Hudson Street, New York, New York 10014

A catalog record for this book is available
from the Library of Congress

ISBN: 978-0-7566-7589-9 (pb)
ISBN: 978-0-7566-7590-5 (plc)

DK books are available at special discounts when purchased in bulk
for sales promotions, premiums, fund-raising, or educational use.
For details, contact: DK Publishing Special Markets
345 Hudson Street, New York, New York 10014
SpecialSales@dk.com

Printed and bound in U.S.A.

Special thanks to:
All the fire fighters at Harrison Street Fire Station, New Rochelle, New York,
especially Danny Heinz, Anthony Costa, and Thomas Connell;
John Santore of Hook & Ladder 5, and the fire fighters of Engine 24 and
Hook & Ladder 5, New York City. Thanks also to Liz Radin.
The publisher would like to thank the following for their kind permission to
reproduce their photographs. Key: t=top, b=below, l=left, r=right, c=center.
Colorific: Ian Bradshaw 23c; **Jim Pickerell** 12c; **Rex:** Cole 14tr;
Greg Williams 25c; **Tony Stone Images:** James McLoughlin 18c.
Jacket images: *Front:* **Dorling Kindersley:** Bergen County, NJ, Law and
Public Safety Institute b. **iStockphoto.com:** Dave Logan t.

All other images © Dorling Kindersley.
For further information see: www.dkimages.com

A WORLD OF IDEAS:
SEE ALL THERE IS TO KNOW

www.dk.com

Fire Fighter!

Written by Angela Royston

It is busy at the fire house
even when there is no fire.
Liz is checking the hoses.
She wants to make sure
they screw tightly to the truck.

Dan is polishing the fire truck wheels.

Anthony is upstairs in the kitchen, looking for a snack. He is always hungry! Suddenly a loud noise makes him jump.

Ring! Ring! Ring!

It is the fire alarm
Anthony slides
down the pole.
THUD!
He lands hard.
But the thick
rubber pad
on the ground
cushions his feet.

Ready for action

Pants are kept rolled down over boots to save time. That way the fire fighters can be dressed and in the fire truck in 30 seconds.

Liz jumps into her boots and pulls up her fireproof pants. She checks the computer. It shows the fire is at 7 Oak Lane. In the truck Liz grabs the walkie-talkie. "Chief Miller! We're on our way!"

"Right!" says the
fire chief.
He has gone ahead
in a special fast car.
"I'll meet you there."

Liz starts the engine
as the fire fighters jump in.
She flips on the sirens and lights
and drives out of the fire house.
The truck speeds toward the fire.

Cars and buses stop and wait
when they hear the sirens coming.

The fire chief calls Liz.
"I'm at the fire scene.
It's an old house
that's been empty for years.
But someone saw a young boy
playing on the porch this morning.
He might be inside the house.
Tell Dan and Anthony to
get their air tanks ready."

"Okay, Chief," says Liz.
"I can see the smoke from here.
We'll be there in two minutes."

Liz turns the corner into Oak Lane.
Flames cover the top of the house.

The fire is spreading quickly.
There's no time to lose!

Hoses

Water comes out
of a fire hose
hard enough to
knock a person down.

Liz hooks a hose from the truck
to the nearest fire hydrant.
A pump on the truck pulls water
from the hydrant to another hose.
Liz and another fire fighter
point the hose at the flames.
"Ready!" calls Liz.

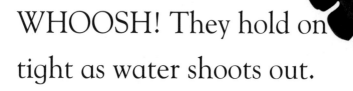

WHOOSH! They hold on
tight as water shoots out.

Breathing equipment
Fire gives off deadly smoke.
Fire fighters wear air tanks
and breathing masks inside
a burning building.

Anthony and Dan are ready
to search the house.
They have put on their
air tanks and face masks.
Each tank holds 40 minutes of air.
That's not much time!
"The boy's name is Luke,"
the chief tells them.
"Right," says Anthony.
   He grabs a hose.
   "Let's put the wet stuff
   on the red stuff!" says Dan.

Dan and Anthony run
to the back of the house.
The fire is not as bad here.
Dan feels the back door.
If it is hot, flames could leap out.
"It's cold," says Dan.
They step inside.

Thick black smoke is everywhere.
Anthony shines his flashlight around.
"Luke! Luke!" he calls.
No one answers.
"I can hear fire upstairs," says Dan.
The fire has damaged the staircase.
It could fall down at any time.
They climb up the steps very slowly.

Outside, the outriggers are set down on the ground.

Outriggers are like legs.
They keep the truck steady
as the ladder is raised.
The ladder goes up
like a telescope
to the top of the house.
A hose runs up the side.
The fire fighter on the ladder
shoots water down on the fire.
The flames crackle and hiss.
They get smaller, then suddenly
jump even higher.

Inside the house, the fire rages.

It is hot enough to melt glass.

Anthony sprays water on the flames.

Fire has made the house weak.

"It could come down any second,"

says Dan. "We must find Luke."

BOOM!

A beam crashes down near them.

But their helmets protect their heads.

CRASH!

"Quick!" says Anthony.

"We're running out of time."

Hard hats
Fire fighters' helmets
are made of hard plastic.
A wide brim helps to keep
sparks off their necks.

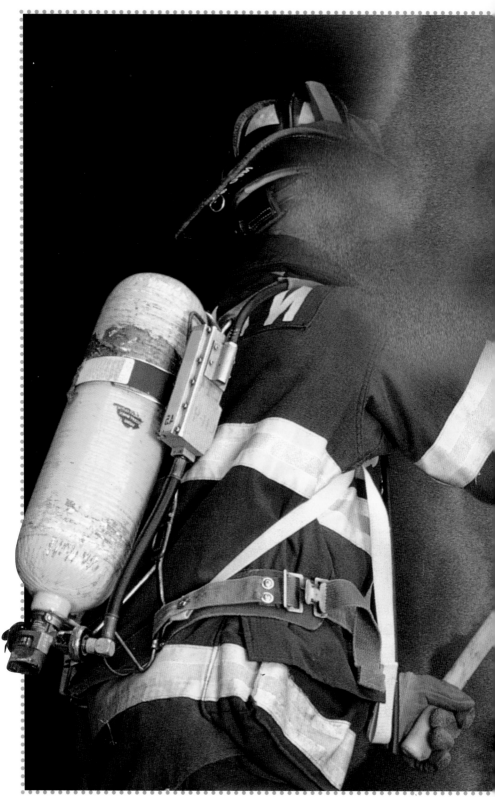

They come to another door.
But it will not open.
Dan swings his axe at the door.
Once. Twice. Three times.
"It's jammed!"
shouts Dan.
The roar of the
fire is so loud they
can hardly hear.
"We'll have to use
the electric saw."

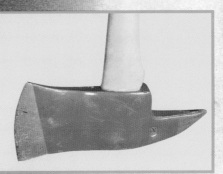

Fire fighters' axe
Axes have been
used by fire fighters
since the earliest days
of fire fighting.

Sharp cutter
The electric saw
runs on batteries.
It can cut right through
the roof of a car
like a can opener.

Anthony switches on the saw.

WHRRR!

He cuts a hole in the door

big enough to climb through.

"Luke!" calls Dan. "Luke?"

But the room is empty.

Suddenly the
chief calls.
"Get out now!
The roof is
coming down!"

Dan and Anthony race downstairs. They get out just as the roof falls in. "We didn't find Luke!" yells Dan. "He's okay," says the chief. "We just found him up the block." "Whew!" says Dan. "Good news!"

Hours later
the flames
are out.
Anthony sprays
water on the
parts still
glowing red.
He is tired
and dirty—
and very hungry!

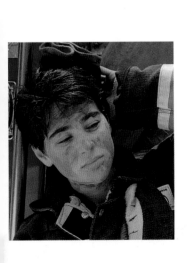

Liz winds
the hoses back
on to the truck.
Finally she rests.
She is tired too.

Back at the fire house
Anthony sits down to eat.
"At last!" he says.

Suddenly a loud noise
makes him jump.
"Dinner will
have to wait!"
laughs Dan.

Ring!
Ring!
Ring!

Practice E.D.I.T.H. – Exit Drills in the Home

Do you know what to do
if a fire starts in your home?
Don't wait until it happens:

- Sit down with your
  family now.
- Talk about how you
  would get out of
  the house.
- Plan at least two ways
  out of every room.
- Decide where you
  will all meet once
  you get outside.

**A fire drill now
could save lives later!**